COOL CAREERS

IN SPORTS

BY AUDRA WALLACE

SCHOLASTIC INC.

Dedicated to Sean and Ryan

contents

Introduction

If you play sports, you've probably dreamed of becoming a famous professional athlete one day. And with a lot of practice and hard work, it could happen! But there are many jobs in sports out there that might interest you, too. Some will get you close to the action on the field, court, mat, or ice, such as working as a coach or a referee. Others will put you behind the scenes, where you'll help injured athletes or invent new sports equipment. There are also plenty of sports jobs in the media industry. You might find yourself interviewing your favorite athlete or editing game footage for live TV. Whatever your passion, if you're dedicated to sports, there's a job out there for you. This book will describe a bunch of them. As a bonus, this book will also introduce you to experts in the field. They'll give you the insight and advice you need to pursue a path to your dream job. So hurry up and read on. It's game time!

CHAPTER 1

PROFESSIONAL ATHLETE

A sports team huddles in the locker room. They've trained and competed almost every day of their professional lives. Now they're ready to bring home the trophy in front of the entire world. Together, they march down a long hallway into the stadium as the crowd chants the team's name.

AT A GLANCE

Job category: on the field
Types of employers: major and minor league organizations
Top qualities: determination, charisma, exceptional talent at playing a specific sport, agility

5

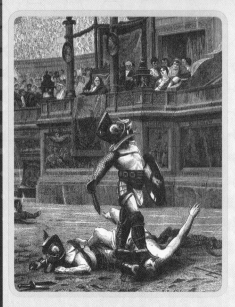

They explode onto the field like fireworks launching into the sky. They're professional athletes. The field is their stage—and the audience is waiting.

A BIT OF BACKGROUND

Athletes have been performing for the public since ancient times. Some of the first were Roman gladiators. These armed fighters often battled to the death in giant **amphitheaters**. These fierce combatants were the sports stars of their day. Crowds cheered on the most powerful and skilled of them. Details about their victories were scratched or painted on plaster walls. Kids even played with gladiator action figures carved from clay!

Today's professional athletes earn money for playing sports. They play on teams that are part of professional leagues. **Spectators** pay admission fees to watch them compete in sporting events. Some professional athletes, such as golfers, tennis players, and boxers, are not part of a team. They compete in tournaments to win prize money.

ON THE JOB

As a pro athlete, you must not only love the sport you play, you must excel at playing it. You'll be paid to compete in and win games for your team or yourself. Competition is tough. Your coach will instruct you on tactics and plays, but it's up to you to make them happen in the game.

THIS JOB IS RIGHT FOR YOU IF . . .

- The rain is pouring and the wind is howling, and you're still outside honing your skills.
- Your favorite days of the week are when your school team has practice.
- Instead of playing games on your computer, you're outside playing pickup games with friends.

TEAM GENERAL MANAGER

Instead of playing for your favorite team, you'll be in charge of it. You'll hire coaches and players, oversee contracts and salaries, promote your team to fans and businesses to make money, and manage your team's budget.

Hours of training and exercise are necessary to improve your skills and stamina. And forget chowing down on pizza, burgers, and fries. A nutritious diet of fruits, vegetables, and high-protein meals will be essential to fueling your performance.

Being a pro athlete requires a big commitment, too. You'll work more than 40 hours a week during your sport's season—and often during the evenings, weekends, and holidays. This includes traveling to and from games, practicing, memorizing new plays, reviewing footage of your competition, and, of course, signing autographs!

EDUCATION

Individual training sessions, team practices, and constant competition are what's in store for you if you plan to go pro. A degree isn't necessary, though most professional athletes earn a high school diploma. Many athletes strive for good grades in the hope of getting recruited by top colleges and universities. There, they'll gain valuable experience and have a chance to showcase their abilities to team owners.

by the NUMBERS

According to the US Bureau of Labor Statistics, there are about 12,000 professional athletes and sports competitors in the United States.

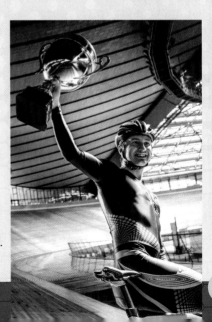

Eric Law

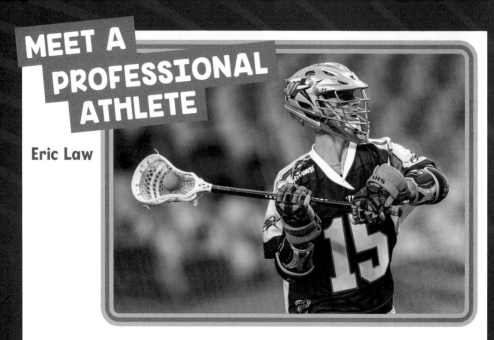

How did you get interested in lacrosse?

When I started playing lacrosse I was six years old. I have two older brothers that both played lacrosse and I wanted to be just like them. I always went to their games and begged my parents to let me start playing as soon as possible.

What team do you play on? What is your main position?

I currently play attack on Atlas, a Premier Lacrosse League team.

Who or what inspired you to become a professional lacrosse player?

I have always looked up to professional lacrosse players and had the dream as a kid to play lacrosse at the highest level. All of my idols were professional lacrosse players and I wanted to follow in their footsteps. Then my college coach pushed me to follow my dreams by giving me the confidence to know I was good enough to play at that level.

What do you enjoy most about playing lacrosse?

Competing with teammates and all of us working together for one common goal. To me, there is no better feeling than working hard and having the freedom to be creative within the game. Lacrosse is a team game, and the best part of being on a team is the relationships that you build over working as hard as you can for something bigger than yourself.

Describe the proudest experience of your career so far.

The most exciting and proudest I have been in my career has been winning three Major League Lacrosse championships with my former team, the Denver Outlaws.

What qualities do you think a person needs to have to be a successful professional athlete?
Someone who can be great at time management and who is very driven and dedicated. It is not going to be easy and is going to take a lot of hard work, and those who are dedicated and love the process of getting better are the ones who are the most successful!

What advice do you have for kids who want to be a professional athlete when they grow up?
Never give up on your dreams and dream big! Work extremely hard outside of the normal practice times and work on your own individual skills. Also try multiple sports and different activities. Playing multiple sports teaches you different aspects of every sport and you can learn important skills from other sports that translate very closely to one another. Enjoy the process!

GAME ON!
Which professional athletes play the most games each season? Check out this graph to find out!

PROFESSIONAL LEAGUE	NUMBER OF REGULAR SEASON GAMES
Major League Baseball	162
National Basketball Association	82
National Hockey League	82
Major League Soccer	34
National Football League	16

CHAPTER 2

SPORTS ENGINEER

AT A GLANCE

Job category: science and technology

Types of employers: sporting goods companies and manufacturers

Top qualities: creative, inventive, problem solver, curious

Whether you're a **novice** tennis player or an expert golfer, part of honing your skills as an athlete revolves around the tools you use. From bats and balls to protective gear and footwear, every sport has its own equipment. Players are constantly looking for products that will help them take their performance to the next level and protect them from injury. It's up to sports **engineers**

to craft new designs using the latest **technology**.

A BIT OF BACKGROUND

For thousands of years, people have been using the basic resources around them to invent sports equipment. Some of the first balls date back to ancient China. People there played a soccer-like game called cuju (also known as tsu-chu). They made a ball out of animal skins and filled the inside with fur or feathers. The ancient Olmec, Mayans, and Aztecs, who once ruled parts of Mexico, created a game known as pitz. The goal was to get a heavy rubber ball through a stone ring. The rubber for the ball came from the milky sap-like fluid of a tree. In Africa, Ethiopians carved curved sticks and balls out of eucalyptus branches and roots to play genna. This sport is similar to field hockey, and is still played there.

As different sports spread around the world, the equipment people created to play them evolved, too. Wood and leather is still used. But different types of plastics, ceramics, fabrics, and metal are also found in the sports equipment athletes compete with today.

ON THE JOB

If you're obsessed with trying out new sports products, and excel in math and physics, becoming a sports

THIS JOB IS RIGHT FOR YOU IF . . .

- You know all of the different sporting goods brands, from Adidas running shoes to Zoggs swimming goggles.
- You make sure your friends' protective gear is secured before a match.
- Your favorite birthday present is new sports equipment.

. . . .

SPORTING GOODS STORE OWNER

Instead of inventing or improving sports equipment, why not be in charge of selling it? Most sports equipment is sold in sporting goods stores. Consider managing or owning one! You'll respond to customer questions and help them find, decide on, and buy a variety of sports products. You'll also supervise staff, keep track of sales and budgets, and build relationships with people in your community.

engineer might be the perfect fit for you. Your job will be to come up with an idea to solve a problem or improve an existing product. For example, do you want to develop a swimsuit that helps swimmers glide through the water faster? Or maybe a better bicycle frame to help cyclists ride safely over rough uphill terrain? Once you have an idea, you'll sketch out how the product will look and function. Next, you'll develop a **prototype** and test it for flaws using computer simulators and real-life situations. Different climates, environments, game scenarios, and body types are just some of the factors that you'll need to consider. Whatever product you invent, you'll need to convince a company to sell it. So prepare to research well and be persuasive!

by the **NUMBERS**

Sporting goods store sales in the US amount to more than $45 billion each year!

EDUCATION

Take all of the science, math, and computer programming courses you can. Physics is a must! Aim to get a bachelor's degree in mechanical engineering. Your courses in mechanical engineering will teach you about how things move. You'll learn how to apply the principles of motion, energy, and force to design and build an object that helps solve a problem.

MEET A SPORTS ENGINEER

Atiqah Shahrin

Describe the job of a sports engineer.
Sports engineers apply mathematical and scientific knowledge and technology to solve sports problems. The two main aspects of the industry are to work with athletes for performance improvement or injury prevention and rehabilitation, or to design equipment. One example is to create football helmets that better withstand impact to keep athletes safe.

Who or what inspired you to become a sports engineer?
I have always loved sports! Growing up I participated in any sport I could, like basketball, soccer, swimming, and badminton. I also had great interest in the sciences, such as physics and biology, and mathematics, so I knew that I wanted to pursue a career in engineering. Engineers are problem solvers and I wanted to apply my knowledge in a field that I was passionate about, which led to becoming a sports engineer. I am inspired to make sports more safe but also exciting and enjoyable for all.

What are some of the projects you've worked on?
One exciting project I worked on was to make better soccer balls. I had to collect information on a ball such as heaviness and roundness. With this information, I experimented with how a ball could fly more smoothly through air. I got to play with a ball launcher that can shoot a ball as far as 90 yards, almost the length of a football field.

Describe your work environment.
My "office" is a mixture of a traditional office, laboratories, and sport facilities. A lot of time is spent thinking and researching, which is done at my desk. However, once I have solutions to the problem, I perform testing either in the lab with machines or with athletes in their natural environment, such as a tennis court or running track.

What are some of the tools you use to conduct research? How do they help you learn about the product you are creating or testing?
Computer-aided engineering is the use of computer software to solve

problems and conduct research. Using this tool, I am able to simulate real-world situations at my desk! I can see how high a basketball will bounce, how hard a tennis ball might accidentally hit someone, or when a baseball bat will crack. With a simulation, you can push your idea to the limit.

What is the most challenging part of your job?
The most challenging part of my job is to be innovative and creative. There are many problems in sports engineering and I must be able to think outside the box. A solution that worked in the past may not work again.

What experience is necessary to become a sports engineer?
Experiences in problem solving are necessary to become a sports engineer. Playing with puzzles and Legos are great ways to exercise this skill. Having an active lifestyle, such as playing outside, supports understanding the natural mechanics of how things work. All these experiences will help when exploring physical phenomena and designing experiments.

Describe the most exciting experience of your career so far.
My current job involves researching and testing new ideas to create golf clubs. To test the performance of an idea, we have a robot that can swing a golf club even better than a human. The robot can swing with a speed up to 150 mph, which is faster than trains in the US. Using the robot for the first time was my most exciting experience so far.

What qualities do you think a person needs to have to be a successful sports engineer?
Eagerness and willingness to expand and share your knowledge and skills is an important quality to be a successful sports engineer. There is always room to learn. By having more information, you are able to tackle problems from different angles. Not all of your solutions may work so having as many ideas as possible helps. Another key quality is a good work ethic, which is putting in honest and hard work.

What advice do you have for kids who want to be a sports engineer?
Explore your interests and expand your skills in science and mathematics. Having a solid foundation in theory will help when you finally apply formulas and principles to real-world applications. While it is not entirely necessary, experience in sports helps with the practical aspect of the job.

CHAPTER 3

REFEREE

A player zooms dangerously close to the sideline. Her opponent is hot on her tail. Shoulders bump. Feet collide. The ball is knocked loose and bounces into the air. Another player slides into its path. The referee blows the whistle just as she blasts it into the net. He notices that her hand touched the ball—and that's against the rules in this sport. Foul!

AT A GLANCE

Job category: on the field

Types of employers: local sports complexes, high schools, colleges, and professional leagues

Top qualities: quick decision-maker, fair, deep knowledge of the sport and its rules and regulations, excellent vision, confident

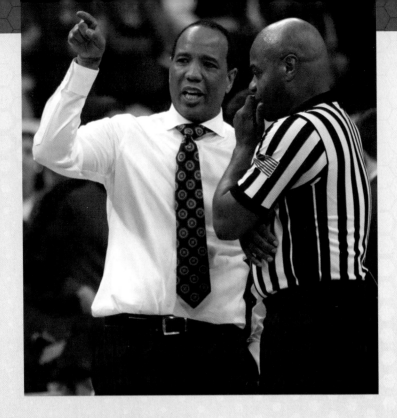

A BIT OF BACKGROUND

Referees enforce the rules of play during a sports competition. It's easy to recognize them because of their uniform. Their black-and-white-striped shirt makes them stand out from the players on the field. Legend has it that a referee named Lloyd Olds invented the famous striped shirt in 1920. Olds often wore a solid white shirt when he officiated at college football and basketball games in Michigan. One day, a visiting football team wore white shirts, too. During the game, the quarterback accidentally handed the ball to him. The player thought Olds was a teammate! Olds wanted to make sure that never happened again. He had

THIS JOB IS RIGHT FOR YOU IF . . .

- You play by the rules—and expect everyone else to.
- You're the kid in the neighborhood who keeps the score during kickball games.
- Your friends always ask your opinion when they're arguing over a play.

Related Career

SCOREKEEPER

When people want to know which team is winning a game, they check the score. Local, national, and professional leagues hire scorekeepers to monitor and update the score, keep time, help track penalties and player statistics, and check the eligibility of players on the roster.

a friend sew him a special striped shirt that he could wear instead. His look caught on and inspired referees around the world. Many referees still wear the stripes today.

ON THE JOB

As a referee, you'll call the shots on the field or court. You'll start and stop the game, keep track of time, count players on the field, allow for substitutions, watch for play interference, and give out penalties when a player violates a rule. You may also inspect sports equipment before or during the game to ensure fair play. In some competitions, you'll judge the performance of players to determine a winner.

Most referees work as a team with other officials. Each one has different responsibilities and often different titles. For example, a professional football game has seven officials. One is a field judge who watches the sidelines to determine whether a player is in or out of bounds. Another is a down judge who sets the **line of scrimmage**, marks the spot where a play ends, and makes calls offside or false-start calls. In baseball, the official is called the umpire.

No matter what the sport, the job of a referee is very stressful. He or she needs to make split-second decisions in fast-paced situations. Players, coaches, and fans will often disagree with your calls, so you'll need to be able to stand your ground. You're also going to run, walk, and stand for long periods of time, so be prepared for an active lifestyle.

EDUCATION

There are no specific educational requirements to become a referee, though you will need to register with your state or local agency. Specific classes and workshops on rules and regulations will help you obtain an officiating license and professional certification. But don't expect to jump right into officiating at the Super Bowl. It takes about ten years of working high school and college games to gain enough experience to be considered by the major leagues.

by the **NUMBERS**
More than 20,000 people work as referees, umpires, or other sports officials in the US.

MEET A REFEREE

Sarah Thomas

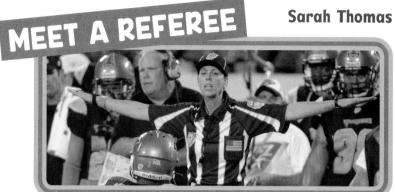

What is your job title?
I am a line judge or down judge (formally known as head linesman).

Who or what inspired you to be a referee?
I've always been involved with sports and wanted to give back. My brother started officiating first. He inspired me.

Why football?
Why not is not what I thought. I never knew there were not any females in football. And considering I'm competitive, I saw learning the game was a challenge to want to learn it all.

How long have you been a referee?
I started officiating in 1996 at a high school in Mississippi.

What is your favorite part of the job?
Being with a crew of officials. All of us working together as a team to be perfect!

Describe the most unbelievable experience of your career.
So far, it was when Kyle Rudolph, a football player on the Minnesota Vikings, accidentally ran into me during a game. It was December 24, 2016, and after my kids knew I was okay, they said, "Mom, you got ran over by Rudolph on Christmas Eve!"

What was your proudest?
Walking on the field for my first NFL game! (In 2015, Sarah Thomas became the NFL's first female official. In 2019, she became the first woman to officiate an NFL playoff game.)

What advice do you have for kids who want to be a referee when they grow up?
Go after it. Work. Don't feel entitled to the job just because you show up. Get started early. High school kids can officiate at local youth sports.

CHAPTER 4

SPORTSWRITER

They're always listening, watching, and asking questions. They know the names of every player, coach, and ref, the history and rules of the sport, and the best spots to watch the game. Their fingers quickly tap out the latest news on a keyboard—and you anxiously await their every sentence. They're sportswriters—and they make the action they see come alive as words on a page.

AT A GLANCE

Job category: media
Types of employers: newspapers, magazines, television networks, online media companies
Top qualities: curious, observant, patient, persistent, good listener, ability to write in a clear and descriptive way

A BIT OF BACKGROUND

Sportswriters report on sporting events. They also describe and reflect on the effects that sports and athletes have on society. Newspapers in the US first began covering sports in the 1830s. They featured the occasional article on a horse race or boxing match. But it was the growing popularity of another sport that hit the field of sports journalism out of the park. In 1862, the *New York Herald* hired Henry Chadwick to report on baseball games. He's considered to be the first full-time sportswriter. Sports columns in other newspapers soon followed.

About 25 years later, *The Sporting News* was published. This weekly baseball magazine was the first publication completely devoted to sports.

THIS JOB IS RIGHT FOR YOU IF . . .

- You're already making a name for yourself as a reporter for the school newspaper.
- Your favorite part of a newspaper or news website is the sports section.
- You constantly carry a notepad around to jot down your ideas and observations.

It became must-read material for not only fans, but players and coaches. *The Sporting News* later expanded to include articles on football, hockey, and basketball. It set the stage for other sports-based publications, such as *Athlon Sports and Life*, *Sports Illustrated*, and *ESPN Magazine*.

ON THE JOB

A typical week for a sportswriter involves watching games and describing what happens during them. You'll write about who's playing well—and who isn't, good and bad calls by the refs, the mood of the coaches, and anything that else that will bring the game to life for your readers. Interviewing sports figures is also part of the job. You'll weave the best quotes into your reporting and research.

Related Career
. . . .
SPORTS ANNOUNCER

If you love talking about sports and have dreams of being on television or the radio, become a sports announcer. You'll announce starting lineups, provide audiences with statistics and play-by-play commentary, and interview players. Get started now by turning down the volume of a game. Practice reporting and commenting on the action in front of your family and friends.

Sometimes, instead of just reporting on a game or event, you'll pitch an idea to an editor of the publication you work for. For example, sportswriters often profile specific athletes, give a behind-the-scenes look at a team, or analyze the strengths and weaknesses of a coach. They are also hired to write scripts for broadcasters to read on television. Some are broadcasters themselves.

EDUCATION

A bachelor's degree in journalism, with a concentration in sports journalism, is preferred. But don't limit your education just to sports. Classes in English, history, science, and other subjects will help you strengthen your storytelling ability, sharpen your research skills, build your knowledge about the world, and enrich your articles. In today's fast-paced multimedia world, knowing how to develop articles with video, photos, audio, and graphics are essential, too.

by the NUMBERS

The most popular sports magazine is *Athlon Sports and Life.* It has more than six million subscribers.

MEET A SPORTSWRITER

Andrew Lawrence

What inspired you to be a sportswriter?
I grew up in Chicago during the '90s and got totally swept up in the excitement of the Michael Jordan-era Bulls. The more I read about them in the newspapers, the more it seemed like the only people having as much fun as the players on the team were the reporters following them around and observing them up close.

What is your favorite sport to write about?
Tennis, because it isn't as stat-obsessed as other sports. You can sit back and appreciate it for what it is: a grand drama full of twists, turns, and complex personalities. It's like boxing without all the violence.

How have things changed since you first started working as a sportswriter?
When I started, there was an understanding that sports figures needed the media to tell their stories. But thanks to the growth of social media, athletes have a say in how they are defined. However, I feel that a writer can explain things about an athlete that they may not fully understand or appreciate about themselves. Those revealing moments make for great stories.

Where do you typically work?
My office is basically my laptop, my phone, and my backpack. Sometimes I work from home, at a local library, or a coffee shop. Other times, in hotel rooms, in airport terminals, on planes, in cars. Sometimes I work from inside the chaos of an actual sporting event. It varies by the assignment.

Describe one of the best experiences of your career.
That would have to be the time when former Chicago Bears head coach Lovie Smith invited me to his house on a football Sunday to watch all the NFL games. It was really rewarding to write about that experience and share it with so many people.

What advice do you have for kids who want to be a sportswriter when they grow up?
Do it. You're going to watch the games anyway. Might as well get paid for it!

CHAPTER 5

PHYSICAL EDUCATION TEACHER

AT A GLANCE

Job category: education
Types of employers: schools, camps, after-school sports programs
Top qualities: athletic, patient, organized, adaptable

Most teachers depend on books and worksheets to instruct their students. But not physical education teachers. Their tools are whistles and stopwatches—and they're not afraid to use them. It's their job to help each student who enters their classroom—the gymnasium—get physically fit. From jumping jacks to push-ups, they know pretty much every exercise routine there is. They're also familiar with the rules of more than a dozen sports and are prepared

to teach them to any student who walks through their doors.

A BIT OF BACKGROUND

If you're reading this book, one of your favorite classes at school is most likely PE. This popular subject got its start in the early days of humankind. Knowing how to climb, throw, jump, and swim were essential to survival. These skills were necessary for hunting food and traveling long distances across rough and often unknown terrain.

In ancient times, warfare was also commonplace. Children as young as seven were trained in wrestling, javelin throwing, and riding horses. These activities would help them develop into strong soldiers.

PE has come a long way since then. By the mid-1800s, it began making its way into schools across the US. Today, most kids take part in a PE class about twice each week.

Related Career FITNESS INSTRUCTOR

Athletes aren't the only people who want to stay in shape. Your city or town probably has a few spots where people, including kids, go to work out or hone their skills at a specific sport. Help motivate them as a fitness instructor. You can teach them yoga, karate, or swimming. Whatever you're good at!

ON THE JOB

The role of a PE teacher is to instruct kids how to exercise, play different sports, and make healthy choices when it comes to the care of their bodies. You'll be responsible for demonstrating exercises, maintaining gym equipment, and keeping records on student progress. Your lessons will help kids safely develop their strength, skills, agility, and coordination. You'll also encourage individual success and teamwork.

EDUCATION

A bachelor's degree—preferably in physical education, **kinesiology**, physical therapy, or nutrition and health—is the minimum education requirement for PE teachers. A state-issued teaching certificate or license is also required. Some states require a master's degree for middle, high school, and college teachers.

by the NUMBERS

The US Department of Health and Human Services recommends that kids age 6 to 17 years should have 60 minutes or more of physical activity each day.

MEET A PHYSICAL EDUCATION TEACHER

Joanne Wetter

Who or what inspired you to be a physical education teacher?
I originally went to college to become an accountant or a math teacher. But I realized that I didn't want to sit behind a desk for a job. Growing up, my favorite period in school was physical education. I also played soccer, basketball, and softball. My PE teachers and coaches always encouraged me to stay active and improve my skills. I decided that I wanted to do the same for other kids.

What is a typical day like?
The job of a physical education teacher is to maximize physical activity time within the class period. I have to effectively organize space, equipment, and my students. Provide equipment that allows all students to be active at the same time. I structure my class so that learning occurs while students are active. My classes are about 40 minutes and I have up to eight classes each day.

How many students do you teach at once?
I am responsible for about 30 students. Though sometimes I team up with other physical education teachers to instruct about 90.

What game is your favorite to teach?
Hula Huts! Kids work as a team to earn hula hoops by throwing dodge balls into a ring or barrel. Each team uses hoops to build a hut or a fort. At the same time, they have to protect their hut from opposing teams who are busy throwing balls at their hut, hoping to knock them down. The team that has the most Hula Huts built when the teacher blows the whistle is the winner.

Why is it your favorite?
It teaches kids how to work together to achieve a goal. It gives kids who aren't athletic a chance to get involved and feel successful, too. There is

a scorer, builder, gatherer, protector, and destroyer, so
there's a role for everyone. The game is also great
for improving physical abilities like throwing
and hitting targets, as well as building
communication and problem-solving skills.

What is your "office" like?

Most of the time I work in the gymnasium. I
also use the outdoor fields for fitness testing.

What is the most challenging part of your job?

It's tough to motivate students that don't like physical
activity. But my job is to find a way—and I love the challenge!

What's the best part?

When I see my students achieve their goals! At the start of the school
year, some kids don't think they could ever run a mile or complete a
certain number of sit-ups or push-ups. By the end of the school year,
they realize just how much they can accomplish by practicing and
working hard. They gain confidence. I'm proud to be part of making that
happen for them.

CHAPTER 6

SPORTING EVENTS PLANNER

The championship game is about to begin. After weeks of countless meetings and phone calls, everyone's hard work is about to come together. Suddenly, the Hall of Famer who was supposed to throw out the first pitch calls in sick. At the same time, the stadium lights begin to flicker and the family members of a star athlete lost their VIP passes. The sporting events planner makes some calls. Whatever can go wrong, will go wrong. Sporting events planners are always prepared.

AT A GLANCE

Job category: public relations and marketing
Types of employers: stadiums, sports facilities, colleges and universities
Top qualities: detail oriented, multitasker, problem solver, good communicator, strong time-management skills

A BIT OF BACKGROUND

People have been holding sporting events for thousands of years. One of the most famous sporting events in history is the Olympic Games. The ancient sports festival began around 776 BCE in Olympia, Greece.

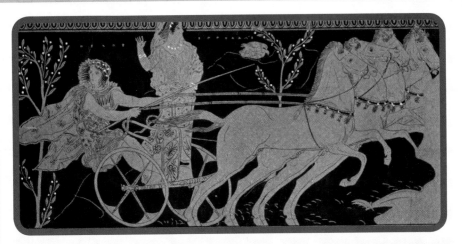

Athletes competed in activities such as foot races, chariot races, jumping, spear throwing, wrestling, and boxing. For centuries, thousands of people traveled to Olympia to see the Games. Gyms, stadiums, racetracks, and guesthouses were built to support the popular event.

Today, the Olympic Games are one of the biggest sporting events in the world. And it's not limited to just one city. This international competition is held in a different place every four years. During the Summer Olympic Games, athletes from around the globe strive for gold medals in sports such as swimming, gymnastics, and cycling. During the Winter Olympic Games, they vie for the top spots in sports such as skiing, snowboarding, and curling.

Other major sporting events include the World Series, the Super Bowl, Wimbledon, and the World Cup. These events attract fans from all over the world.

THIS JOB IS RIGHT FOR YOU IF . . .

- You volunteer to organize and run fund-raisers.
- Your friends would describe you as dependable.
- You'd rather produce the school play than star in it.

ON THE JOB

A sporting events planner is in charge of every detail that goes into preparing a sporting event. Whether it's a college track meet or a

Related career

STADIUM MANAGER

Sporting events planners often work hand in hand with stadium managers. They are in charge of the day-to-day operations of a venue and supervise all of its employees. Some of your tasks will include establishing safety rules, setting prices for products and services, hiring staff, maintaining the cleanliness of the facility, negotiating contracts with food companies, and promoting the stadium for events.

professional wrestling match, your goal will be to make sure that the teams have what they need to perform, the fans enjoy themselves, and the facility is up and running. The sports organizations and the airports, hotels, and restaurants near the event will depend on you to help them shine—and earn them **profits**.

A typical day for you might include reviewing press releases, strategizing how to promote an event on social media, or booking a celebrity or sports star for an appearance. Part of your job will also involve setting up transportation and places to stay for teams and staff members, coordinating security, and overseeing schedules, budgets, and sales.

EDUCATION

The sports industry is a business, so you'll want a bachelor's degree in business. You'll need to understand budgets and have a solid background in contracts, sales, and marketing. Degrees in communication, public relations, and event management are also useful since a lot of your time will be spent interacting with the press, players, celebrities, and the community.

by the **NUMBERS**

Imagine being a sporting events planner for the Summer Olympics. In 2016, more than 10,000 athletes from more than 200 nations competed in it!

MEET A SPORTING EVENTS PLANNER

Jacqueline Secaira-Cotto

What was the first sporting event you ever attended?
I went to a New York Yankees game at the age of five. It was Roy White Bat Day and I was at the game with my dad and older brother. Both of them influenced my love of sports. The Yankees won and I got my own baseball bat to take home.

How did you get your start as a sporting events planner?
I started in finance. But after six years, I decided that it was time to pursue a career in an industry that I had a passion for—sports. I completed a master's degree in sports management, and landed an **internship** with the New York Knicks. Afterward, the Knicks hired me full time.

What is your current job title?
I'm Major League Baseball's Director of Special Events.

What is your favorite part of the job?
I love to meet people in the different cities that we travel to, whether it is for an All-Star Game or the World Series. There are so many people involved in putting together a spectacular event. It is a team effort!

Describe one of the best experiences of your career.
I served as the Venue Chief for a World Baseball Classic tournament in Miami. Puerto Rico played the Dominican Republic. It was a highly competitive game, in a sold-out stadium filled with fans who cheered louder than any other game I had witnessed. The tournament celebrated the diversity of the game and the brotherhood of the sport with both teams being from Latin American countries.

What advice do you have for kids who are interested in this type of job?
If your passion is sports, do all you can do to learn every day, read as much as you can, meet as many people as you can. Volunteer, intern, and hustle. I think it's important to pick a career in an area that you love. It should not feel like "work." If you are passionate about it, you'll get to your dream job. I did.

CHAPTER 7

SPORTS TALENT AGENT

AT A GLANCE

Job category: public relations and marketing; law

Types of employers: professional athletes, coaches, and other sports figures in the spotlight

Top qualities: competitive, persuasive, outgoing, organized

You know the names of all the top athletes who play your favorite sports. You've memorized their stats and watched every game they're in on TV and online. Their names and images are on your clothing, sneakers, and sports equipment. But how did they get to the top? Often it's because a sports talent agent recognized their talent—and got that talent in front of the right people.

THIS JOB IS RIGHT FOR YOU IF . . .

- You're a natural negotiator.
- You have a knack for talking other kids into playing what you want to play.
- You're friends with all the basketball players even though you're not on the team.

A BIT OF BACKGROUND

The biggest responsibility of sports talent agents is to get the best deals for their clients. Those clients are mainly professional athletes and coaches. The job of the sports talent agent got its start in 1925. That's when movie theater manager Charlie Pyle **negotiated** a contract for a talented college football player named Harold Edward "Red" Grange. At the time, pro football players only earned between $25 and $100 per game—if they were paid at all! Pyle got the popular halfback $3,000 per game with the Chicago Bears, plus a cut of the money made on tickets. One game could earn Grange as much as $20,000! Later, Pyle helped

Charlie Pyle

Harold Edward "Red" Grange

Grange score **endorsement** deals that put his name on a candy bar and a sporting goods line.

Over time, the sports industry boomed into a big business—and so did the role of the sports talent agent. Nowadays, most professional athletes have one.

ON THE JOB

As a sports talent agent, you'll seek out talented sports figures to represent. Once you find them, you'll try to convince them that you're the right person to promote and guide their careers.

Much of your time will be spent on the phone negotiating their salaries with teams who want to recruit or retain them. Once they're employed, you'll help them get endorsement deals with **sponsors** who

ReLated career SCOUT
· · · · · · · · · · · · · · ·
You might have an eye for talent but have no interest in reading contracts or making deals. Look into the job of scout. You'll travel around the country to high schools and colleges, searching for skilled athletes. Professional leagues will depend on you to spot the top up-and-coming players to recruit for their teams.

want their names and faces to advertise their products. Think Nike, Adidas, and Under Armour. Image is everything, so you and your staff will also review press releases, social media, and branded content for your clients. Arranging interviews and coordinating your clients' schedules is part of the job, too.

Professional athletes have short careers compared to other jobs. There is constant competition and a high risk of injury. Good sports talent agents prepare their clients for careers after they retire from a sport. For example, some professional athletes go on to become coaches, broadcasters, or business owners.

EDUCATION

Many sports talent agents have law degrees. Though not required, the ability to review and understand contracts is a key part of the job. Classes in finance, public relations, accounting, marketing, and sports management provide aspiring agents with a solid overview of the industry. Many states also have licensing requirements. This is to make sure that agents know and follow the rules when it comes to recruiting clients, especially student athletes.

If your goal is to represent football players, the National Football League Players Association requires a postgraduate degree. Be prepared to pursue either a master's degree in business administration (MBA) or a juris doctor (JD), the first degree in law.

by the NUMBERS

In 2018, the highest-paid athlete was boxer Floyd Mayweather. He earned $275 million for one match!

MEET A SPORTS TALENT AGENT

Eugene Lee

What sports did you play as a kid?
I played every sport under the sun. My first love was playground football during recess at St. Michael's School in Canton, Ohio. I was a quarterback and I loved calling plays, throwing the ball, and leading the action.

What inspired you to become a sports talent agent?
I met my first clients playing pickup basketball while I was in law school at Notre Dame. My friendships with these football players awakened within me a genuine desire to guide, protect, and support their professional careers.

What is the most challenging part of the job?
The extensive travel and time commitment are the most grueling parts of the job. To do your job well, you need to develop and maintain relationships nationwide. You also need to be ready, willing, and able to address and resolve client-related issues as they arise.

Describe the most exciting experience of your career.
One of the most exciting moments of my career occurred when I had clients on both the New York Giants and New England Patriots in Super Bowl XLVI in Indianapolis, Indiana. My brother came out to attend the game and it was an unbelievable experience, one that I'll never forget.

What qualities are necessary to become a sports talent agent?
You need to be a self-motivated hard worker with excellent interpersonal communication skills and the resilience to keep getting back up after being knocked down. This industry is not for the faint of heart. That said, if you stay the course and believe in yourself, you will come out victorious in the end.

What advice do you have for kids who want to be a sports talent agent when they grow up?
Take ownership of your dream, even at a young age. There is absolutely nothing in this world that can prevent you from being whatever you choose to be if your talents and passions unite.

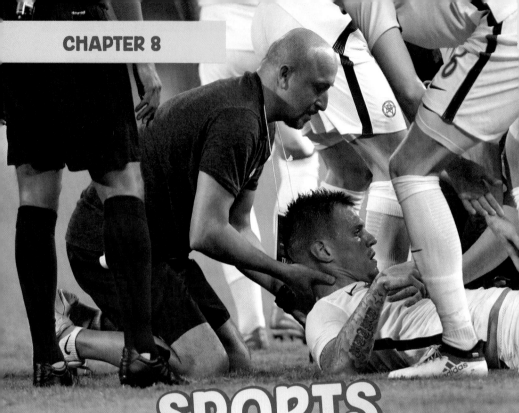

CHAPTER 8

SPORTS MEDICINE PHYSICIAN

A hockey player twisted her knee. A track star sprained his ankle. A pitcher can't move his shoulder. Who will help them? A sports medicine physician, that's who!

Sports medicine physicians are experts in assessing injuries that occur during sports activities. They

prevent, diagnose, and treat a variety of conditions that affect human bodies on the move.

A BIT OF BACKGROUND

The field of sports medicine can be traced back to the ancient Olympics. The rise of athletes in Athens, Greece, fueled the need for *gymnastes*. These early athletic trainers helped people improve performance and prevent injury through exercise. One of the most famous was Herodicus, who is considered to be the "father of sports medicine." Hundreds of years later, a Greek doctor named Galen served as "team physician" at a school for gladiators. He treated their battle wounds and stressed the importance of proper diet, rest, and cleanliness.

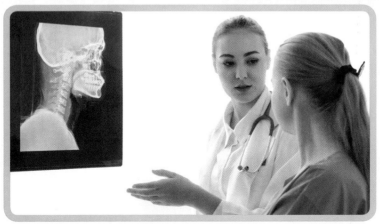

ATHLETIC TRAINER

Medical school is a big commitment. But don't let that discourage you. You can still help people without becoming a doctor. Teams often hire athletic trainers to provide first aid in emergency situations, help athletes prevent injury, and develop fitness programs.

ON THE JOB

As a sports medicine physician, you'll examine athletes for injuries to muscles and bones. Common injuries include fractures, sprains, and dislocations. You'll check their bodies for redness, swelling, and tenderness, and test muscle strength and joint movement. Ordering and interpreting **diagnostic** tests, such as X-rays, may be necessary. These tests allow you to see inside the patient's body. After the examination, you'll recommend a treatment plan to get your patient out of pain and back in the game.

If you're certified as an orthopedic surgeon, you'll operate on patients. For example, knee injuries are common in sports. If a **ligament** tears, you will go into the knee to repair it.

A big part of your job will also involve teamwork with other medical experts like physical therapists, nutritionists, and athletic trainers. They will put your treatment plan into action by helping your patient build strength, eat healthy, and prevent further injury.

EDUCATION

The career path for a sports medicine physician starts with a bachelor's degree and premed classes in **anatomy**, biology, and chemistry. You'll then need to pass the Medical College Admission Test (MCAT) to gain entrance into a four-year medical school. At medical school, you'll continue your education in the study of the body and get hands-on experience with patients. Once you earn your doctor of medicine (MD) or doctor of osteopathic medicine (DO) degree, you'll apply for a license and complete a primary care residency. A residency is when you work for a hospital or clinic under supervision. Next, you'll continue your training with a fellowship or specialty training program. During your fellowship, you'll focus on sports injuries and treatment. Finally, you'll take an exam to become officially certified in sports medicine.

by the **NUMBERS**

In the United States, more than 30 million kids participate in sports.

MEET AN ORTHOPEDIC SPORTS MEDICINE SURGEON

Dr. Oladapo Babatunde

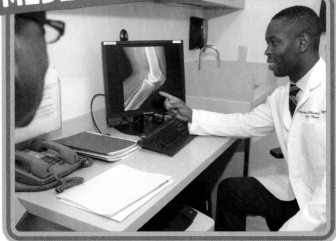

What does an orthopedic sports medicine surgeon do?
An orthopedic sports medicine surgeon is dedicated to treating athletic injuries of the musculoskeletal system, with a special focus on shoulder, elbow, hip, knee, and foot and ankle injuries.

Who or what inspired you to become one?
I played sports all my life and enjoy working with athletes and active people. The patients that I see are injured or have a problem that stops them from performing. It's rewarding to be able to fix their problem and help them regain the ability to return to sports or work.

What is your favorite part of the job?
Helping patients to regain function and the ability to perform as they were before. Whether it's someone who returns to the football field or a mother who can now lift up her child, our treatments can often be life changing. The proudest times are when patients have great outcomes.

What is the most challenging part of the job?
One of the biggest challenges of the job is that results take time. After surgery, patients must often go to physical therapy to regain their function and return to playing.

What advice do you have for kids who want to pursue this career?
Follow your passion and work hard to become better every day at it. If you focus on this, you will not only find success but also happiness and fulfillment.

CHAPTER 9

COACH

Every team has a coach. Some have two or more. You'll often spot coaches pacing the sidelines, checking their clipboards, and glancing at the scoreboard. You'll hear them cheering—or reprimanding—players, calling for substitutions, and disputing penalties with the referees. They are the chief motivators, trainers, and organizers of a team.

AT A GLANCE

Job category: on the field; education

Types of employers: middle schools, high schools, colleges and universities, local sports clubs, amateur and professional leagues, athletes who want to sharpen their skills

Top qualities: ability to lead, organized, observant, strong communication skills, inspiring

BIT OF BACKGROUND

The word "coach" came about in an unusual way. It originated in a Hungarian village called Kocs. During the 1400s, people in the village transported goods in a special horse-drawn carriage that was invented there. This wagon was called a *kocsi*, or coach. It offered smooth rides and stability when making turns. Word about these wagons spread throughout Europe. Over time, "coach" became a metaphor for a tutor who helps "carry" students through an exam. Later, it took on another meaning—an instructor who helps carry athletes to victory.

Kocsi

THIS JOB IS RIGHT FOR YOU IF . . .

- Your teammates follow your lead on the field.
- You're known for sketching out plays on napkins, paper plates, or whatever you can get your hands on.
- You're the one who rallies your team through a loss and leads them in a chant to inspire a win.

Related Career

ATHLETIC DIRECTOR

Many cities, towns, and schools offer extracurricular sports, clinics, and summer camps. They need athletic directors to run them. Use your knowledge of fitness and sports to manage their teams and programs. You'll set up rosters, hire and oversee coaches and referees, keep track of the budget, and schedule practices and games.

ON THE JOB

As a coach, prepare to lead a team through the good and the bad. You will be in charge of developing your players into the best they can be.

You'll instruct them on the rules of the game, model proper technique, run practices and training sessions, and choose plays that will help your team defeat an opposing team. Knowing the strengths and weaknesses of your players will help you find ways to improve their performance. You'll devise specific drills around the skills they need to work on, individually and as a team.

Not all coaches instruct teams. Some work with individual athletes in sports such as golf, tennis, swimming, and figure skating. But no matter what sport you want to coach, good sportsmanship and a strong competitive spirit will get you far.

EDUCATION

A high school diploma is preferred. Most professional coaches earn a bachelor's degree in subjects like physiology, kinesiology, physical education, or sports medicine. Some people who coach school teams also work as teachers at the school. Teachers are required to have a bachelor's degree in education and state certification.

MEET A COACH

Natalie Nikase

What sports did you play as a kid? What were those experiences like for you?
I played basketball, volleyball, track, and cross-country. I loved playing team sports because I enjoyed working together and beating my friends. I always wanted to win so I tried my best.

Who inspired your career path?
My father did because he was the one who taught me basketball. He was so passionate about the sport. I believe his passion became my passion.

What was the first team you coached? What was the most important lesson you learned from it?
The first team I coached was my AAU team called HOOP4LIFE. I learned that I couldn't teach competitive spirit. It's either in your DNA or not.

How has your past experience as a basketball player influenced your job as a coach?
My experience as a basketball player was what made me become a coach. Coaching became an easy transition because I was able to make adjustments on the fly and attack opponents' weaknesses. It also gave me a commanding voice, which I felt very comfortable using to direct teammates and eventually players as a coach.

What is your favorite part of the job?
Feeling my players gain confidence and watching their progression. I'm obsessed with the idea of improving and progressing on a daily basis.

What advice do you have for kids who want to coach one day?
Helping and serving people is one of the best feelings in the world and I think anyone can coach if they have a big heart. Work on having an open mindset. You'll need to be able to communicate and work with all different kinds of people. Don't be afraid to ask a lot of questions to coaches with more experience and make sure to find a good mentor.

CHAPTER 10

SPORTS PRODUCER

A truck sits quietly outside a stadium. But it's no ordinary truck. Inside it's bustling with activity. Headsets buzz with updates from the rink. A wall of monitors, big and small, glows in the darkness. The sports producer's eyes dart from one image to another to another. Announcers clutch their microphones. Players skate onto the ice. Crowds of people rush to their seats. Camera operators line up their shots. 5-4-3-2-1 . . .

AT A GLANCE

Job category: media
Types of employers: local and network television stations
Top qualities: ability to make quick decisions, anticipate, communicate, and lead

A BIT OF BACKGROUND

If you're like most fans, you watch live games on TV. But years ago, most people either attended games or listened to them on the radio. Then, on May 17, 1939, the way people saw and heard sports changed in a big way. On that day, NBC aired a baseball game between two college

THIS JOB IS RIGHT FOR YOU IF . . .

- You're rarely without a camera and pretty much film everything.
- You watch games for player and crowd reactions, not just the best plays.
- You ask your parents for tickets to sporting events instead of video games for your birthday.

teams—Columbia and Princeton. It was the first time that a sporting event was televised in the United States. A camera on a 12-foot platform filmed the action from the third-base side of home plate. The game was viewed on only about 400 TV sets. But it was a history-making moment that helped boost the popularity of TVs. Nowadays, millions of people around the globe watch sporting events on TVs, computers, and mobile devices.

ON THE JOB

A sports producer is in charge of all the action people see on their screen during a game. A typical day might include attending the teams' morning practices and meeting with players and coaches to find out as

Related Career
. . . .
VIDEOGRAPHER

Are you handy with a camera and known for getting the best shots? Do you already spend most of your time watching sporting events? Look into becoming a sports videographer. You'll capture footage of practices, games, tournaments, and interviews for local and national TV stations and online broadcasts.

much information as you can about the day's competition. You'll also touch base with announcers to discuss what they plan to talk about during the event. Reviewing footage and news articles from previous games will keep you up-to-date on stats and possible storylines. After some rehearsals with your crew to check equipment, you'll document all the action during the game.

A key part of your job will be to decide what you'll show during the stoppage of play. You might replay something that just happened, put up game stats, show crowd reactions, or have the announcer tell a story about a player or reflect on a play.

Some sports producers work in a studio on TV shows like *SportsCenter*.

The World Cup is the most-watched sporting event in the world. In 2014, more than 1 billion people viewed the final match!

They mainly broadcast news, scores, drafts, and highlights from a variety of sports competitions.

EDUCATION

Most sports producers have a bachelor's degree in broadcasting, communications, or journalism. Courses on camera operation, lighting, sound, and editing will help you develop the skills you need to work in this multimedia field. Many colleges have a radio station, website, and newspaper that cover the school's sports teams. Some have relationships with local and national TV stations, where you can apply for an internship.

MEET A SPORTS PRODUCER

Chris Ebert

What are some of the sporting events you have produced content for?
I've been lucky enough to have produced just about every sport imaginable, from college field hockey and water polo to NHL Hockey and college football and basketball. I have worked on five Olympic Games and two Super Bowls. And I've also worked on the Running of the Bulls (and yes, I've run with them—three times!).

What is your favorite part of the job?
My favorite part of the job is my favorite part of sports—every day is different and you never know what is going to happen. Every game is a different set of teams and athletes in a different city with a different set of storylines—and it all happens in real time. It keeps everything fresh and exciting.

What is the most challenging part of your job?
The most challenging part of the job is covering the live action and deciding what the viewer wants to see or should see. When the action is happening so fast and furious and you only have a few seconds to decide what to put on the air—that is the most challenging—and also the most fun!

Describe the most exciting experience of your career.
Being able to work on the opening and closing Olympic ceremonies as well as track and field at the home of the Olympics in Athens, Greece. Also, producing the NHL All-Star Game from one of the meccas of hockey, Montreal. With all of that franchise's history and the legends that were in attendance, it's something I'll never forget.

What advice do you have for kids who want to get started in the field?
The best advice I can give is to learn everything. I worked at the college radio station calling games as well as being a music DJ. I interned not only in the sports department but running camera, teleprompter, and the switcher. By the time I was producing, I knew how everything worked and the importance of everyone else's job around me. The more you can do, the more doors you can open.

conclusion

Now that you've learned all about these cool careers in sports, what do you want to be when you grow up? Don't worry! You don't need to decide right now. Instead, have fun playing and learning about sports with your family and friends. Here are some activities to get you started:

- Join different teams to experience working together with others to achieve a goal.
- Play multiple sports to learn the ins and outs of different games, experience different styles of players and coaches, and strengthen your own athletic abilities.
- Volunteer to coach or officiate at local games at a camp or a sports facility.
- Read books and news articles about the history of different sports and their impact on society and culture.
- Support your local sports teams by attending games and writing news articles about their games.
- Watch videos of top athletes, coaches, and referees to deepen your knowledge of your favorite sports.
- Interview people in your community who already work in sports, like coaches, refs, physical education teachers, and store owners. They may have a tip or two for you, or even let you watch them do their jobs.

No matter what career you're interested in, get outside and play. You never know what you might discover about yourself, others, or the game!

organizations

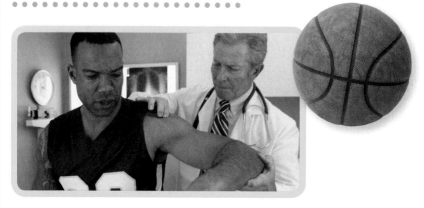

American Orthopaedic Society for Sports Medicine
9400 W. Higgins Road, Suite 300
Rosemont, IL 60018
847-292-4900
www.sportsmed.org

National Academy of Sports Medicine
1750 E. Northrop Blvd.
Suite 200
Chandler, AZ 85286-1744
800-460-6276
www.nasm.org

National Alliance for Youth Sports
2050 Vista Parkway
West Palm Beach, FL 33411
1-800-688-5437
www.nays.org

National College Athletic Association (NCAA)
700 W. Washington Street
PO Box 6222
Indianapolis, IN 46206-6222
317-917-6222
www.ncaa.org

Special Olympics
1133 19th Street NW
Washington, DC 20036-3604
202-628-3630
www.specialolympics.org

The United States Olympic Committee
One Olympic Plaza
Colorado Springs, CO 80909
719-632-5551
www.teamusa.org

WEBSITES JUST FOR YOU

Exploratorium
www.exploratorium.edu/explore/sport-science

Safe Kids
www.safekids.org/sports

Sports Illustrated Kids
www.sikids.com

SPORTS BY THE NUMBERS

PROFESSIONAL MAJOR LEAGUES IN THE US

NAME OF PROFESSIONAL LEAGUE	YEAR FORMED	NUMBER OF TEAMS AS OF 2019
Major League Baseball (MLB)	1903	30
Major League Lacrosse (MLL)	2001	6
Major League Soccer (MLS)	1996	24
National Basketball Association (NBA)	1949	30
National Pro Fastpitch (women's softball)	2004	6
National Football League (NFL)	1920	32
National Hockey League (NHL)	1917	31
National Women's Hockey League (NWHL)	2015	5
Women's National Basketball Association (WNBA)	1996	12

Other professional sports organizations include the Professional Golfer's Association (PGA), Ladies Professional Golfer's Association (LPGA), United States Tennis Association (USTA), and Worldwide Wrestling Entertainment (WWE).

Michigan Stadium

TOP 10 BIGGEST SPORTS STADIUMS IN THE US* (BY CROWD CAPACITY)

STADIUM	LOCATION	CAPACITY
Michigan Stadium	Ann Arbor, MI	107,601
Beaver Stadium	University Park, PA	106,572
Kyle Field	College Station, TX	102,733
Tiger Stadium	Baton Rouge, LA	102,321
Ohio Stadium	Columbus, OH	102,082
Neyland Stadium	Knoxville, TN	102,038
Bryant-Denny Stadium	Tuscaloosa, AL	101,821
Darryl K. Royal-Texas Memorial Stadium	Austin, TX	100,119
AT&T Stadium	Arlington, TX	100,000
Sanford Stadium	Athens, GA	92,746
Rose Bowl	Pasadena, CA	90,888

*As of 2018

Names To Know

Meet some groundbreakers who have made a big impact in the world of sports.

Alberto Riveron

ALBERTO RIVERON
1960-

Alberto Riveron is the NFL's first Hispanic referee. Riveron's family moved from Cuba to the US when he was five years old. He grew up in Miami, Florida. While most of his friends played soccer, Riveron preferred football. He began officiating youth football games as a teenager. He later moved up to college games as a field and side judge for the Big East conference. The NFL hired him as side judge in 2004 and promoted him to referee in 2008.

Chloe Kim

CHLOE KIM
2000-

Chloe Kim is the youngest half-pipe snowboarder to win an Olympic gold medal. Under the guidance of her dad, the California native started snowboarding at four years old. At 17, she took home the gold at the 2018 Olympic Winter Games at PyeongChang in South Korea.

Edith Houghton

EDITH HOUGHTON
1912–2013

Edith Houghton is considered to be Major League Baseball's first female talent scout. The Philadelphia Phillies hired her in 1946. At the time, the team was at the bottom of the league. Houghton helped strengthen their roster for six years while she worked a second job at a hardware company. Houghton's other claim to fame was being recruited by the Philadelphia Bobbies, a semipro women's baseball team. She became their starting shortstop at just 10 years old!

MARK MCCORMACK
1930–2003

Mark McCormack is considered to be the pioneer of sports marketing. As a young lawyer in 1960, he represented a rising golf star named Arnold Palmer. McCormack made a deal for Palmer to endorse golf equipment for Wilson Sporting Goods. His success with Palmer and other sports stars led to the creation of the International Management Group

Mark McCormack

(IMG), the world's largest athlete representation firm. IMG went on to become the largest independent producer of TV sports programming. It also promotes and manages hundreds of sporting events throughout the world. *Sports Illustrated* once called him "the most powerful man in sports."

PAT SUMMITT
1952–2016

Pat Summitt was an American women's college basketball coach. She won more games in basketball history than any other man or woman, and was the first NCAA Division I coach to reach 1,000 victories. Summitt

Pat Summitt

started her career at the University of Tennessee in 1974 when she was 22 years old. By 2003, Summitt had led her team to a record-breaking 800 wins. She also coached the US women's basketball team at the 1984 Olympic Games and took home the team's first-ever Olympic gold medal. In 2000, the legendary coach was inducted into the Naismith Memorial Basketball Hall of Fame.

SHERYL SWOOPES
1971–

Sheryl Swoopes was the first player to be signed in the WNBA. The Houston Comets recruited her in 1997. She played with the Comets for 11 years, where she earned more than 2,000 points and four championship wins. Swoopes is also a three-time Olympic gold medalist and the first women's basketball player to have a Nike shoe named after her—the Air Swoopes.

WENDELL SMITH
1914–1972

Sportswriter Wendell Smith began working at the *Pittsburgh Courier*, the nation's largest African American newspaper, in 1937.

Sheryl Swoopes

Through his columns, he spoke out against segregation in professional sports. At the time, white players and black players did not play on the same teams. Smith's efforts led Branch Rickey, the manager of the Brooklyn Dodgers, to sign the first black Major League Baseball player—Jackie Robinson.

Glossary

amphitheaters: large buildings with seats rising in curved rows around an open space on which games and plays take place

anatomy: a branch of knowledge that deals with the structure of organisms

diagnostic: relating to identifying a disease or injury from its signs and symptoms

endorsement: the act of official approval and support

engineers: people who plan, design, and build

internship: the position of a student or trainee who works in an organization, sometimes without pay, in order to gain work experience

kinesiology: the study of how the human body moves

ligament: a tough band of tissue that holds bones together or keeps an organ in place in the body

line of scrimmage: the imaginary line separating two teams at the beginning of a play

manufacturers: makers of products

negotiated: discussed with another so as to arrive at an agreement

novice: a person who has no previous experience with something

profits: money made from sales

prototype: an original model on which something is patterned

spectators: people who watch an event

sponsors: companies or organizations that pay the cost of a radio or television program

technology: machinery and equipment developed from the use of scientific knowledge to solve problems

ABOUT THE AUTHOR

AUDRA WALLACE graduated from Ithaca College, where she studied communications and elementary education. Her passion for writing nonfiction and teaching kids led her to a position with Scholastic. Since 2006, Wallace has written and edited the award-winning classroom magazine *Scholastic News* Edition 3, as well as nonfiction books for the Scholastic Library Publishing Group. She is also the author of *Cool Careers With Animals*. According to her kids, Audra is also pretty good at soccer and throwing a football.